EUROPA ⚔ MILITARIA No36

WARSAW PACT BADGES

RICHARD HOLLINGDALE

THE CROWOOD PRESS

First published in 2011 by
The Crowood Press Ltd
Ramsbury, Marlborough
Wiltshire SN8 2HR

www.crowood.com

British Library Cataloguing-in-Publication Data
A catalogue record for this book is available from the British Library.

ISBN 978 1 84797 281 1

Dedication
This book is respectfully dedicated to the memory of Reginald 'Don'
Billows: friend, collector, a fair and honest dealer of antique militaria.

Acknowledgements
Grateful thanks goes to my partner Alexandra Vígh for her help,
support, and encouragement during the writing of this book.

Designed and typeset by Focus Publishing, Sevenoaks, Kent
Printed and bound in Singapore by Craft Print International Ltd

Foreword

Lenin said that military service was the sacred duty of every citizen. That may have been so in the USSR, but in Socialist Hungary the mood was slightly different. For those who remembered the fearful days of 1956 there was a lingering sense of disappointment towards the army. (People felt that the majority of the Hungarian People's Army had been set against them when they had been most in need of its protection.) For the younger generation, conscription was unpopular for more straightforward reasons. Military life was strict with very little leave, food and conditions were basic, and the punishments often harsh and frequently applied. As a whole, the experience came as a shock to many young men. My husband was a dog handler for the state border guards in the 1970s and he was treated little better. He was often sent out at night on lone patrols along the Yugoslavian border looking for smugglers. On one occasion he caught an escaped murderer on the run from Czechoslovakia, for which he received extra leave.

Not everyone disliked military life, though. My father was a career soldier and enjoyed the fruits of a more beneficial system. He was very proud of his military service and was happy to have served his country. I was very young at the time and the details are now vague, but I do remember that he kept a pistol on top of the wardrobe, which scared me very much. One thing we did not fear, though, was the West. Those with a simple grasp of politics saw the USSR as a genuine protector of the people and, whether we believed the propaganda or not, with a generous welfare system and no unemployment, we all felt secure in our lives. Only those with a greater knowledge of politics or a memory of the state security forces during the 1950s carried any sense of fear, but they were a minority until quite late in the history of the Peoples' Republic. Only when the economic collapse of the country became imminent in the 1980s did people as a whole really face the reality that socialism was failing.

Now that Hungary is a democratic country it seems strange to have cause to dwell on the past. Most especially, it seems strange that the relics of the socialist regime have become collectors' items. We in Hungary have long looked upon them as trash and we have all been guilty of discarding much of it over the past twenty years. (I threw away all of my husband's old badges a long time ago.) In an odd way, therefore, it makes me happy to know that these items are now being acquired by foreign buyers, as I am flattered that people from other lands should take an interest in our history. We have spent a long time forgetting this part of our heritage, so it may well be good that these foreign collectors are helping to remember what otherwise may have become lost. My only concern is that they remember it in the correct way. They did not experience the life we called our own and I fear that they have an idealistic view of the events and politics that dictated our every movement for forty years. I had a happy childhood, but as an adult I can see that it was a time that brought not only great security but also great sadness into our lives. For those who died in the struggles of 1956, or generally suffered at the hands of the state security forces, it is the sadness that we should remember most of all.

Nelly Vigh
Pécs, Hungary
September 2010

Contents

a separate star riveted to the badge's main body. Air force and airborne officers also had a change of insignia, although their version had the M55 mounted on a laurel wreath and was worn on the peaked cap and beret, replacing an earlier type with just a red star at its centre. The remaining head-dress, those items requiring insignia, made use of the same M55 badge used by the army. In the field, an identical olive drab painted pattern was worn. On those occasions it was the additional arm-of-service piping to the general's field service cap that identified his superior status. On the peaked cap of the air force and airborne troops an additional wing device was also worn, which consisted of outstretched wings mounted by a gold star. Of interest, this same device was also adopted by the CSSR, Bulgaria and Hungary (the latter having silver for other ranks and gold for officers). The final addition for the officers was the M69 parade insignia. It had the M64 oval

as its centre piece surrounded by a laurel wreath encircling it and reaching out at right angles along its base. Generals and marshals wore a similar version, except theirs had the M64 oval surrounded by a wire embroidered wreath on a felt base. Naval officers wore their own cap badge on the peaked cap and *ushanka* (seaborne and support services) and beret (naval infantry), which had an anchor as its centre piece and came in two colours: gold and silver. The gold badge was worn by seaborne officers and naval infantry, while the technical support services, such as administrative personnel, medical and engineers, wore the silver version. The officer navy badge was distinctive in that the crowning red star contained the hammer and sickle device within a white circle. Early examples were made of brass and enamel or wire embroidery, to be replaced in 1964 by a painted aluminium version, which was worn on all occasions.

(**Above**) USSR Soviet Armed Forces general and officer quality subdued cap badges (various manufacturers). The far right example is a modern copy.

(**Above**) USSR Soviet Armed Forces other ranks cap stars (left to right): M64 painted aluminium, standard type and superior quality examples, subdued field service.

(**Above**) A very young Soviet Navy conscript photographed in 1981. He wears a Baltic Red Banner Fleet ratings cap with the M69 other ranks insignia. Although it carried the designation model 1969, in reality, it would not have been universally worn until 1971. Due to the immense size of the Soviet Armed Forces any planned changes could only ever have been phased in over a number of years.

(**Above**) A family of three Soviet conscripts photographed during the 1970s. The central man is in the artillery, although he wears an armoured crewman's protective helmet. Most likely, he drove an armoured personnel carrier used to transport a gun crew. The men to left and right wear the M69 other ranks and NCO's cap insignia (left) on the *ushanka* winter hat and (right) parade peaked cap. All three men wear slight variations of the winter uniform.

When the M64 star was not used by other ranks and NCOs of the armed services they employed the M69, a large-sized red star surrounded by a golden laurel wreath (rare examples of which were a two-piece construction). This badge saw service within the field on the beret and *ushanka*, as well as the service dress and parade peaked cap. For sailors it was worn on the rat-ings cap and *ushanka*, with the exception of the naval infantry. These soldiers had their own insignia, which they wore on their black berets, comprising of a red star on a black, oval field surrounded by a coil of golden rope. As with the *Spetznats* (airborne paratroops) the naval infantry paraded in their berets and so had no change of insignia on such occasions.

(**Above**) USSR Soviet Armed Forces air force and airborne wings for wear on the everyday and parade peaked caps. The same cap device was employed by the CSSR, Hungary and Bulgaria.

(**Right**) Yugoslavia – commonly mistaken for Soviet badges, the Yugoslavian People's Army employed a very similar range of badges. The example shown is for an officer and would have originally come with a silver-painted aluminium star burst backing plate. Other ranks cap stars can be distinguished by the fact their edges were angled (whereas the Soviet version was flat) and that they came in both silver and gold.

Bulgaria

Other ranks and NCOs wore a plain red star on their head-dress (25mm), initially made of brass and enamel, later painted aluminium and thin enamel paint. During the early 1980s, for the *ushanka* and berets, the other ranks' traditional insignia (which was retained on the side cap) was replaced by a gold lion mounted on a red star surrounded by a golden wreath measuring 35mm × 31mm. This badge, like the former, was made of painted stay-bright. In addition to these insignia, the side cap and beret also had a small cloth shield featuring the national colours placed on the wearer's right-hand side.

Although sponsored by the poorest of the Pact nations, the Bulgarian People's Army (BNA) still managed to issue one of the best quality badges worn by any of the Pact nations. The original late-1940s version of the officer's badge was made of white porcelain and enamelled brass, national colours of white, green and red behind a central red star measuring 27mm × 34mm. Later versions were made of painted brass (1960s) and then painted stay-bright mounted on a white plastic oval star-burst (1970s). This was worn on the everyday service peaked cap, *ushanka* and overseas cap. It was replaced in the 1970s by a rampant lion on a red (army) blue (air force) or black (navy) background surrounded by a gold wreath and a star above its head. On parade a different badge was worn. It had a more traditional silver lion as its centre piece mounted upon the national colours and an oval star burst, all of which was framed by a brass wreath (63mm × 45mm).

(**Above**) Bulgarian People's Army officer cap badges (left to right): original M49 pattern brass, enamel and porcelain; 1970s–1980s brass and plastic parade; 1970s everyday and field service.

(**Right**) Bulgarian People's Army officer cap badge, 1960s–1970s plastic variant.

(**Above**) Poland beret badges (left to right): army camouflage and navy. Other versions included a black background for armour; pale blue, naval infantry; burgundy, airborne. Those of officer quality were made from embroidered metal.

(**Above**) A Polish airman photographed during the 1980s. His peaked cap clearly demonstrates the Polish Air Force eagle, recognizable by the *hussar wings* crowning the eagle's head. These *wings* were originally worn on the uniforms of Polish hussars in the seventeenth-century. Since that time they have acquired something of an elite status and so it was an honour for the air force to have them present on their insignia.

Hungary

Hungary had been one of the Axis Powers during World War II. Defeat followed by bankruptcy meant that the newly formed socialist army was forced to employ a combination of surplus German weapons and Soviet uniforms in 1949. In keeping with most Socialist armies of that era, the cap insignia was heavily influenced by the Red Army and came in two forms: service and field dress. The service dress was a large brass and enamel wreath made of ears of corn. The top was crowned by a red star, from which radiated light waves, while the base sported the national colours of red, white and green. The centre featured a crossed hammer and ear of corn on a blue field. Measuring 38mm × 38mm it was of an unusually large size and so was too big for the overseas side cap. Instead, this item of uniform was decorated by a small brass cockade (23mm diameter). Its centre piece, on a pebbled brass field, was an enamelled red star containing the crossed hammer and ear-of-corn motif. The national colours, rendered in paint, decorated the circumference. The badge was equipped with twin holes at the top and bottom so that it could be sown to the front of the cap. This, evidently, proved a bore for many conscripts, as these badges are sometimes encountered with a pin soldered to the reverse side. Both badges were of good-quality manufacture. Their limited production (1949–56) makes them significantly rarer than other Hungarian cap badges and so should be considered a lucky find when encountered in good condition.

In 1957 the Hungarian People's Army (MN) initiated a period of remodelling that it hoped would restore public confidence after the failed uprising of 1956. One attempt to break from the past was to change the cap insignia. The basic design was an oval (29mm × 24mm) and comprised of three concentric rings. The central field featured the national colours, upon which was mounted a red star. Peaked caps, or plate caps as the food-conscious Hungarians call them, were decorated with a stamped metal badge – gold border for generals and officers and silver for NCOs and other ranks. Early versions of the badge (1950s–60s) were decorated by a plastic star, the very earliest of which had a painted field behind. Those of a similar age, but not quite as old, had a coloured field made of an enamel effect plastic. In the 1970s the plastic star was replaced by a one-piece construction with a flat surface, although the red star was designed in such a way as to give it a raised appearance.

For all ranks, the field cap employed a subdued version made of Bakelite. Early versions of this badge were made of a black-brown colour (1950s–60s), while the later versions were a lighter, chocolate brown (c.1965–89). The most common type to be encountered is that of a slightly flat, slim relief. Of a rarer and slightly older kind is a badge with a high relief and pronounced contours. Of final interest is a version that sits between the everyday service dress and field badge. The backing oval was brown Bakelite, while the central piece was a coloured brass and enamel (the only post-1956 Hungarian army badge so far encountered to use genuine enamel). Photographic evidence demonstrates that it was an early form of field service badge used from the late 1950s to mid-1960s, whereupon it was phased out in favour of the plain brown Bakelite field badge.

The Danube Flotilla (principally a border guard defence on water) wore a yellow-gold version of the M57 cap badge with an additional wreath situated above that of the standard insignia. The Worker's Militia wore only one badge, irrespective of rank, a five-pointed brass star (25mm) with red enamel, the quality of which appeared not to have suffered any economic variations over time.

(**Above**) Hungarian People's Army M49 cap badges (top to bottom): peaked cap, field side cap and *ushanka*.

(**Above**) Hungarian People's Army M57 officer cap badges (top to bottom): early issue with plastic star; later issue one-piece construction.

(**Above**) A postcard of a Hungarian conscript wearing the M49 field insignia on his *ushanka* winter hat. The tunic is not of the Soviet-style, so it would place the date at around c.1956–57.

(**Above**) Hungarian Officer Cadet Domonoks (left) and two friends wearing plate hats with the M49 pattern cap badge. (**Kind** permission of Ms Domonkos.)

CSSR

Czechoslovakia was created in the aftermath of World War I from the remnants of the old Austro-Hungarian and German Empires. It was meant to satisfy one of Woodrow Wilson's fourteen points, principally that which concerned self-determination. It was a noble ideal, but in reality the Czechs and the Slovaks had strong individual identities (and rivalries) that were well-established long before 1918. A strong cultural identity, made all the more pronounced by the use of two separate languages, witnessed a disproportionately high ratio of Czechs to Slovaks in the armed forces. One area where a fairer degree of unity was achieved was in the cap insignia.

The first socialist army of Czechoslovakia was established in 1948. Its cap insignia was a Soviet-styled red star within which was contained a silver Czech lion and Slovak coat-of-arms. Made of brass, enamel and silver gilding it was of exceptionally good quality, and was probably reserved for wear on the everyday service peak cap as photographic evidence shows a subdued brass square with rampant lion being worn on the field service side cap. Unusual, for many badges of a similar type, it had the maker's name and location on the reverse in clear lettering. This badge appears to have remained in service until c.1959–60 and measured 32mm. In 1960 the government was confident enough to proclaim that it had achieved socialism and so was ready to progress towards the next stage, communism. As an initial step, a new title was adopted: Czechoslovak Socialist Republic. The consequence for the armed forces, judging from the parallel evidence supplied by academy badges, was to gain a new insignia. In its basic form it was an enamelled pentagon containing a rampant lion embossed with heraldic shield (21mm × 37mm). The socialist star was thus confined to the top most portion of the pentagon above the lion's head. Age determined the quality of manufacture with early examples being a mix of enamel-effect plastic and silver gilt lion, while later examples were painted brass covered by a thick plastic lacquer. An anodized backing plate was also applied on occasions. Certainly the later type was of military origin – an anodized halo of golden sunrays for officers and silver for other ranks, dating from the 1980s – but the remaining two featured in the colour plates are not as well-known to the author. The enamelled patterns were worn on the peaked cap with a plain brass badge applied to the field head-dress and *ushanka*. Additional concealment was supplied by a subdued version, often seen on Paratrooper berets. Unlike other socialist states, all ranks appear to have worn the same badge, as photographic evidence demonstrates no discernable differences. Photographs from the early 1970s suggest that the People's Militia (LM) wore the same badge as the army or no badge at all. However, between 1973 and 1982 an anodized star containing the national coat-of-arms was adopted for wear by the LM.

(Clockwise from top left)

CSSR Czechoslovakian People's Army cap badges (left to right): early version with enamel-effect plastic and silver gilt; later version painted with plastic coating.

CSSR Czechoslovakian People's Army subdued cap insignia.

CSSR Czechoslovakia People's Army later issue cap device with silver-painted aluminium halo. (Slightly rarer than the version with the gold halo.)

Romania

Romania's socialist history was divided into two distinct phases: Romanian People's Republic (1950–65) and the Romanian Socialist Republic (1965–89), both of which produced distinct badges. The primary badge of the RPR was the traditional revolutionary star. It measured 33mm and contained a blue and yellow cockade with the initials RP in the centre. The standard version was made of brass and enamels, either stamped or solid with a two prong attachment. A subdued field version was also worn. Parade helmets were decorated by a large representation of the national coat-of-arms (full colour enamel and brass). This came in two versions: an early type (1950s) without a red star and a later version (1960s) with star measuring 41mm × 46mm. Officers wore a brass wreath with a central enamelled oval within which was contained the RPR star (51mm × 41mm). Generals, in keeping with most other Pact nations, wore badges made from a central enamelled insignia surrounded by embroidered wire. In their specific case oak leaves.

The Romanian Socialist Republic initially continued the tradition of wearing a red star, a good-quality two-piece brass and enamel badge, with the national coat-of-arms rendered in white metal measuring an overall size 39mm. This changed to a more individual style, which remained in place until the end of the regime. Officers wore a twin oak wreath (measuring 50mm × 44mm overall) and NCOs had a single wreath within which was contained a full colour rendition of the national coat-of-arms (40mm × 44mm). Other ranks wore the national coat-of-arms, also full colour enamel, mounted on an oval halo surround (30mm × 38mm). All of these badges were worn on the peaked cap, ushanka, overseas cap and beret. Early versions can be discerned by the quality of the enamel as the lettering is easier to read due to the fact the words *Republica* and *Socialista* were contained exclusively within the yellow band of the national colours. Later badges tended to have the lettering overlapping the national colours, which makes the individual letters more difficult to see. It is also interesting to note the wide variation in colour on the enamel. Air force badges can be identified by virtue of an additional pair of wings extending from either side of a slightly smaller central wreath, which lacked the words *Republica* and *Socialista*. Generals wore a wire-embroidered badge on red felt with an enamelled national coat-of-arms to the centre – identified by the fact that the oval halo was only just slightly larger than the coat-of-arms. For the other ranks, at least, a subdued version was worn in the field (28mm × 35mm). This was a single piece stamped in rugged brass. When on parade, a larger RSR version of the large national coat-of-arms was worn on the steel helmet. Sources are uncertain, but a plain brass helmet badge also appears to have been worn. The metal was wafer thin, but incredibly strong so it would have been suited to the rigours of active service. The Patriotic Guard is said to have worn a near identical set of badges, although photographic evidence is yet to support this assertion and it is possible that these badges were for regular army non-combatants. The only difference appears to have been that the wreath was silver, except for on the beret. The beret badge was the national coat-of-arms (22mm × 26mm) surrounded by a piece of red felt.

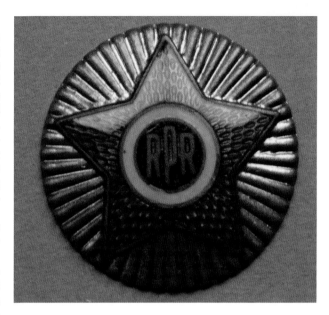

(Above) RPR Romanian People's Army general rank cockade. Originally this badge would have come with a red felt backing that featured a three leaf gold embroidered surround.

(Above) RSR Romanian People's Army other ranks cap insignia (left to right): army; subdued field service; militia (patriotic guard) older type with the more distinct lettering.

(Right) RSR Militia beret badge. This badge would originally have been worn with a red felt backing cloth.

(**Above**) RSR Romanian People's Army officer air force cap insignia. It is interesting to note that the state coat-of-arms is of a smaller size to those found on the army cap badges.

(**Above**) RPR and RSR Romanian People's Army (top): officer collar insignia, RSR white metal and enamel cap badge; (second): RSR other ranks everyday; field; militia; (middle): RSR NCO army; RPR officer; RSR NCO militia; (fourth): RSR officer; RPR general; RSR officer militia; (bottom): general rank collar insignia; RPR army cap badge.

(**Above**) RSR Romanian People's Army parade helmet plate, later type without enamel decoration.

Excellence Badges

USSR

The most common and universally awarded badges issued by the Warsaw Pact armies were those celebrating military excellence. The first army excellence badges were introduced to the Red Army in 1942. Initially, there was a series of seven badges honouring frontline troops, such as sniper, tank driver and machine gunner. These were expanded to include such support staff as engineer, signaller and even baker. The last of the Great Patriotic War (World War II) standard to be introduced was the Excellence in Air Force, established in either 1949 or 1950 (sources fail to agree). Throughout the 1950s these badges continued to celebrate individual trades (identified by the trade insignia on the lower portion of the badge) but these gave way in the 1960s to one of three generic types: army, air force and navy (the army version was also issued to airborne and border guards). The awards were open to other ranks and NCOs and were worn on the wearer's upper right breast, usually in line with the second button down from the neck on the M69 service tunic. Lesser awards extended in a line from the excellence badge towards the shoulder and then below. Only the guard's badge had precedence. If the wearer had an even higher award, which also went on the right side, it was worn above the excellence badge. As a whole, it was a worthy award to have had as it was noted on the conscript's permanent record and so contributed towards their civilian employment file. Interestingly it was an award not exclusively confined to Soviet troops alone. Members of other nations, had they served or trained with the Soviet Army, were also eligible for this award.

The first type (1960s) of army excellence badge featured in this book was made of gilt-finished, painted brass and enamel or just painted brass, while the second type (1970s–91) was

(**Above**) USSR Soviet Armed Forces first type generic army excellence badge made from brass and enamel with painted border, 1960s–1970s.

(**Above**) USSR Soviet Armed Forces second type generic army excellence badge made from painted aluminium, 1970s–1991.

(**Below**) USSR Soviet Armed Forces both early and later type generic army excellence badges without painted border.

(**Below**) Soviet Artilleryman photographed in 1949 wearing one of the wartime trade specific Army Excellence Badges.

made of stay-bright painted aluminium. Both types were a pin back produced by a variety of manufacturers, although the earlier version is encountered as a screw back on rare occasions. Examples from the Great Patriotic War had a screw back so the post-war screw-back versions are presumably from the earliest date of issue. The first type was stamped and had a mirror image to the reverse, while the second type was solid with a smooth or textured reverse and a maker's logo. The 1960s version also comes in two varieties: painted border or plain brass. No explanation for this difference has made itself apparent, although when it occurs on the stay-bright versions, minute scratches demonstrate that the paint has been purposefully removed. The best explanation is that it was a form of unofficial military fashion observed by some soldiers.

(**Above**) USSR Soviet Armed Forces Excellence in Military Construction (left to right): first issue; later issue, note the change in letter size and the simplification of the grenade and sub-machine gun.

(**Above**) Russian Federation. One of the many excellence badges employed by the Armed Forces of the Russian Federation of States in the initial post-Soviet 1991–94 era. The Russian Federation still issues very many excellence badges today.

(**Above**) A Hungarian Munkasor (Worker's Militiaman) wearing the generic Soviet Army Excellence Badge above his Hungarian awards. The photograph dates from the c.1980s and shows the brass and enamel excellence badge with grey painted border.

(**Above**) A Soviet NCO photographed in 1963 wearing the generic Army Excellence Badge with plain brass border. He also wears adjacent to the excellence badge a third class sports badge. Just visible on the right hand side is the Komsomol Youth Pin.

Hungary

Although Hungary was the smallest of the Warsaw Pact armies, it still appeared to have had the widest range of excellence badges. They came in two grades: excellent and outstanding. Each of these could be awarded up to three times. Similar to the wartime Soviet examples, the badges were specifically designated, although the Hungarian versions were not applied to certain trades but particular roles: cadet, soldier, squad leader, platoon leader and so on (see Table for 1969 – 89 type badges opposite).

The first examples issued for the army were between 1967 and 1969. Of good quality, they were made of a sturdy brass and enamel with red painted lettering. The excellence badge had a white border, while the outstanding badge was plain brass; both were graded one, two and three. Such badges are often sold as first, second and third classes. This class distinction is inaccurate as the numeral records the number of times the badge was awarded, consequently making the number three grade noticeably scarcer than the lower two. The reverse was fixed with a twin-claw attachment or, on rare occasions, opposing fingers. In 1969 these badges were replaced by more simplified designs of a smaller size. Early versions of this badge had a flag with heavy enamel-effect plastic, while later issues had a much thinner coating. These badges were awarded according to the designations

previously described. In the 1980s a further alternative with an added wreath (but otherwise more economical manufacture) emerged. These seemed to have dispensed with the system of numbering and were graded according to their inscribed legend and coloured wreath (gold or silver). All of the above badges were available as quarter-size miniatures for off-duty purposes, which accounts for their now comparative rarity as they are quite small and delicate. The 1969 badges were attached to the uniform by the opposed fingers rather than the twin claws.

(**Above**) Hungarian People's Army (left to right): 1967–69-type Outstanding Platoon Leader; Excellent Squad Leader. The numbers indicate the number of times the award was given and not its grade or class.

(**Right**) Hungarian People's Army (top): Excellence Cadet; KTP Sports Badge with gold wreath; Excellent Platoon Leader; (second): KTP Sports in gold; Excellence in Military and Political Training in gold; KTP Sports in bronze; (third): Outstanding Soldier first, second and third awards; (bottom): KTP Sports in silver; Excellence in Military and Political Training in silver; KTP Sports in iron.

DDR

The DDR had what was considered by many Western observers as the most professional non-Soviet army within the Warsaw Pact, so it is a surprise to consider that the NVA had quite a modest range of badges. Of the badges on offer, the NVA excellence badge was awarded for good conduct and the demonstration of sound military knowledge. The first type was the *NVA Leistungsabzeichen* (Achievement Badge) and was employed 1959 – 90. It featured an oval oak wreath that contained the forward profile of a soldier standing before the state flag. It is tempting to speculate that it came in three grades: gold, silver and bronze; but this is not true. Although only issued as a bronze award, it was still a higher order decoration, rated above that of the later qualification clasps given for displays of technical skill.

The first excellence badge of certain date was the *Bestenabzeichen* (Best Soldier Badge) awarded 1964 – 85. The design featured a laurel spray and side profile of a helmeted soldier on a red field, below which the legend read: DDR National Volksarmee. Like its Hungarian counterpart, this version was numbered and repeat awards were demonstrated by the addition of a number hanger – a small attachment at the bottom corner that recorded the number of times it had been awarded. Between the years 1969 and 1982, the number hanger was graded from one to twenty-five, after which, between the years 1982 and 1985, the badge was reduced to just three

awards. In 1986 a final version was produced, which was graded one to four; made of a brass shield, it featured a rifle and bayonet held aloft from which the legend: *Bester* emanated. The field was coloured red for the Army and green for the Border Guards. Of unknown pedigree is a Bester Badge that is said to have been an unissued prototype due to replace the 1986 pattern; but this cannot be confirmed without further research. It may still prove to have been a fantasy piece and collector's would be wise to observe caution when unknown badges make similarly unsubstantiated claims.

The *Kampfgruppen Besten Badge* (Workers' Combat Militia) was of a more modest design. Prior to 1975 it was comprised of a sprig of laurel over which flew a plain red flag and was awarded to the best soldiers and units graded in gold, silver and bronze classes with an oval number plate at its base. Between the years 1975 and 1980, a modified example came into use without a number plate. Its replacement, issued between the years 1980 and 1990, was of the same basic design with the addition of the state coat-of-arms to the centre of the flag and an overall slightly larger size. Multiple awards were not uncommon, so the gold class is the most frequently encountered, which creates the slightly unusual situation where the lower grades are in fact the harder ones to find. Often overlooked by collectors in the past, all of these badges have since acquired a greater level of desirability equal to that of their NVA counterparts. As a consequence, all types and grades should be considered noteworthy finds when encountered. The only flaw they have, which is common to many of the DDR badges, is that the lacquered surface of the badge is very fragile. A slight knock or firm pressure of the thumb can cause the lacquer and paint to come off in fragments or even a single sheet, and great care has to be taken when handling them. The end result, of course, has been to make good-condition examples a rarity and, with an increase in time, this will impact upon their availability and price and so make them significantly difficult to acquire.

(Above) DDR National People's Army (top): 1964 Best Solder, screw back; 1959–90 NVA Achievement Badge; 1965–85 Best Soldier, pin back with hooks for additional number hanger; (middle): 1986–90 Best Border Guard; NVA Sports Award; 1986–90 Best Soldier; (bottom): 1990 prototype Best Border Guard – either a fantasy piece or a possible replacement for the 1986–90 pattern; Best Worker; Warsaw Pact Anniversary pin.

(Above) DDR Worker's Militia (top): Excellent Militia last issue 1980–90 type; second issue 1975–80 in gold, silver, bronze; (second): Worker's Militia Twenty-Fifth Anniversary; complete set of True/Faithful Service medals for the Worker's Militia; Worker's Militia Thirty-Fifth Anniversary; (third): Worker's Militia Thirtieth Anniversary; Civil Defence Best Badge; (bottom): Worker's Militia Marksman, early type with number; Worker's Militia later type Marksman in gold; Parachute Sports; Worker's Militia later type Marksman in silver and bronze.

The Civil Defence and Military Sports Association (BST) were not to be left out. They too issued excellence badges, of which the *Zivil Defence* Badge is the most substantial: brass shield featuring the organization's coat-of-arms and the legend *BESTER* contained within a white strip above. Like the NVA version, the Civil Defence Bester Badge was equipped with a hanger attachment and could have been awarded a multiple of times. The BST Badge was of a more modest design, featuring the organization emblem contained within a red flag beside which stood a sprig of laurel and the initials BST below.

Poland

Like the USSR, Poland had quite an extensive range of excellence badges for what they described as exemplary service (*wzorowy*). Each badge celebrated excellence within a particular trade. The most commonly encountered excellence badge was a generic design graded in gold, silver and bronze, the first version of which came out in 1958. A small rectangular badge or circular (depending on the recipient's status), it featured the side profile of a soldier wearing a Soviet-style helmet, behind which could be seen the national colours. Both the soldier and the border were coloured in accordance with the award status. The legend along the bottom or around the border specified the type of soldier to whom the award had been given. Variations included soldier, border guard and marine. An alternative type was numbered with the relevant numeral featured in the bottom left-hand corner. The 1958 version can be identified by the absence of a laurel wreath on the helmet (featured on all later types). The earlier helmet was also of a higher, more pronounced, shape. All of the numbered badges came in a silver-coloured metal in one of three sizes: off-duty lapel, standard 29mm × 38mm and large 31mm × 48mm. The later version, with wreath, was issued 1973–99. The rarest

(**Above**) Poland Excellent Soldier in gold.

type was issued between the 1950s and early 1970s. Its design was similar to the Soviet types of World War II in that they featured the arm-of-service insignia. The only exception was a generic type (silver eagle in a red shield) labelled: *Exemplary Service*. Those of a specific type carried a legend such as: *Exemplary Cook, Driver* or *Mortar*.

(**Above, top left**) Poland Excellent Border Guard.
(**Above, top right**) Poland bronze class Excellent Student.
(**Above, bottom**) Poland gold and bronze class Best in Service Excellent Badges.

(**Left**) Poland (top): Excellent Soldier in bronze; Armoured Proficiency clasp; Excellent Soldier in silver; (second): Marksman in bronze; ushanka cap badge; Sports Badge in silver/grade two; (middle): Parachute Instructor; Parachute Qualification; Parachute Instructor third class; (forth): Military School Graduation; large-size numbered Excellent Soldier; Military Academy Graduation; (bottom): Excellent Cadet in gold; Excellent Marksman; Excellent Cadet in silver.

Romania

Romania's range of excellence badges depends on how they are viewed. Within the most basic analysis there was a single excellence badge throughout most of its socialist history: a gold shield within which was contained the national colours and the state coat-of-arms. Around these features read the legend: *Militar de Frunte*. It was issued both by the RPR and the later RSR. The only differences being the slightly altered state coat-of-arms and the initials RPR found on the earlier examples. Often of good quality, it was constructed of brass and enamel with a screw back. With only slight variations observable over time (mostly differences in size), the RSR design remained largely unchanged from 1965 to 1989. Earlier badges from the RPR of the 1950s followed the original Soviet pattern and were designated to specific trades until the generic pattern described above was adopted. The table below illustrates a number of those commonly available.

If the survey is extended, other badges also existed that could have been seen as an excellence award. The most commonly encountered, probably due to Romania's mountainous landscape, is the *Alpinist Militar*, awarded to mountain troops in three or four numbered grades. Originally its design was the same as the standard ungraded 1950s badge (almost identical to the Excellence in Infantry except the background colour was green and the legend read: *Vanator de Munte de Frunte*) but its appearance changed during the 1960s and 70s to suit a more individual design. Another contender was the *Tragator de Elita* (elite sniper), which appears to have only been issued in a single class. Like the Alpinist badge it too started off as a standard excellence badge (1950s) before adopting its own individual design (the first of which was issued by the RPR in the 1960s – red shield within which was contained a gold wreath, target and crossed rifles – and a final version produced by the RSR from the 1970s until 1989). Both of these badges were made of solid brass with a pin back. They were of good quality, but the Romanian habit of lacquering badges (also practiced by Hungary and the DDR) has left the latter type looking somewhat worse for wear. The metal has still tarnished below the lacquer, while the lacquer itself reacts with daylight and has turned a shade of brown. The overall effect is to produce a badge rather dirty in appearance. Originally it would have given the badges an enamelled look, but it is sad to see that they do not age particularly well.

Romanian Excellence Badges

Infanterist de Frunte	Infantry
Artilerist de Frunte	Artillery
Art. A. A. De Frunte	Anti-aircraft
Tankist de Frunte	Armour
Vanator de Munte de Frunte	Mountain
Gospodar de Frunte	Legal
Santitar de Frunte	Medical
Constructor de Frunte	Construction

(Clockwise from top right)

RPR Romanian People's Army excellence badges (left to right): Excellent Infantry; generic Excellent Soldier; Excellent Tanker.

RSR Romanian People's Army generic Excellent Soldier badges (left to right): early issue, note how the colour of the enamel matches that of the RPR version; smaller size issue; later issue.

RSR Romanian People's Army Excellent Military Construction.

RSR Romanian People's Army Excellent Mountain Troop class one; Elite Sniper, late issue; Excellent Mountain Troop class two.

Bulgaria

As with Romania, Bulgaria's awards were greatly influenced by the USSR. The early issue excellence badges were just such an example with an almost identical appearance to those awarded by the USSR during World War II. The main differences, though, were to be seen in the addition of the national colours and the fact that the trade insignia and national insignia (hammer and sickle) were in opposite places to the Soviet version. An oval badge also existed, judging from its usual condition and quality from the 1950s, with a large red star and trade insignia surrounded by an oak wreath. How long it remained in circulation is unknown, but its comparative rarity suggests that it was not for very long. Whatever the case, a replacement pattern arrived in the 1960s that followed the design of the new Soviet Army excellence badge issued from 1960 onward, although the Bulgarian pattern appears to have been specific to the semi-autonomous Ministry of Military Transport. As with earlier patterns, a number of small differences did exist between itself and its Soviet parent. The most notable of these changes was the addition of the national colours and alternative setting of the trade insignia, which was placed at the top of the badge rather than at the bottom. Across the front of the badge was a red banner containing the Cyrillic legend: *Excellent*. Later versions were much the same only with a reduction in quality and manufacturing complexity, being made of a more economical single cast painted aluminium. Of a similar type was the award for Excellence in Combat & Political Training, which can be seen as a generic all-purpose replacement to the individual trade badges described above. This badge featured representations of the party and national flags, below which was an enamelled assault rifle and open book. Across the lower third was the customary banner and legend, although the colour of the banner varied depending upon which grade the badge was: red for class I; green, class II; white, class III. This was reduced in the 1970s to a single ungraded award. Like standard army excellence badges, the Excellence in Military and Political Training Badge went from being a brass and enamelled award to painted aluminium. A higher version was reserved for ranks of colonel and above, noticeable by virtue of its increased size. The inscribed banner came in two colours: standard red and a much rarer pale blue.

(**Above**) Bulgarian People's Army Excellence in Military Construction. This was one of many types and was issued to members of the semi-autonomous Military Construction, a corps of men made up of personnel otherwise unfit for full military service.

(**Above**) Bulgarian People's Army Excellent in Military Training Competition Winner.

(**Above**) Bulgarian People's Army (top): Parachute Qualification with loops for additional number hanger; Excellence in Military and Political Training, senior version for higher ranking officers; Parachute Qualification –] standard type; (second): Excellence in Military and Political Training (left to right): graded version; generic brass and enamel; generic painted brass; last issue generic painted aluminium; (third): Military School Graduation –] reserve officer; Warsaw Pact Annual Manoeuvres Participant's Celebration Badge; Military Officer Academy Graduation; (bottom): Ministry of Military Transport excellence badges (left to right): early issue with brass and enamel – two-piece insignia missing; painted brass; last issue painted aluminium.

CSSR

As with every other award issued by Czechoslovakia, it would seem, the excellence badge is quite elusive when compared to the neighbouring states. There could well be many still in circulation within the Czech Republic and Slovakia, but they only seem to appear on rare occasions in the UK. As such, there is very little to say other than to give a brief description of the examples that existed. The first type was a simple wreath supporting an enamelled red star within which was featured the heraldic lion surrounded by a white ribbon that contained the appropriate legend: *VZORNY TANKISTA* (good/excellent tank) for example. Below was the trade insignia. These early badges were made of stamped brass and, on occasions, had a numbered plate attached to the reverse. The border guards had their own version featuring a border guard surrounded by the legend: *ZAVLAST-ZA SOCIALISMUS* (on green ribbon) *VZORNY POHRANICNIK* (on white). The base was decorated by the border guard's heraldic wolf's head.

As with the other nations described, the army and air force badges were replaced by a generic award featuring the side profile of two servicemen – airman and soldier – with two crossed Roman swords at the base (the same device stamped on clothing and field equipment). Around the soldiers was an enamelled white or blue ribbon bearing the legend: *VZORNY VOJAK*. The white ribbon was found on the earlier type two badge and the blue on the latter type three (brass and enamel) and type four (painted aluminium) badges. An alternative version, identified by dealers as an excellence badge, was a rectangular badge made of painted aluminium. A simple, yet attractive design, it sported the national colours on a vertical axis with a red star at the top and a gold wreath a half to two-thirds down towards the base, meant to celebrate the *VZORNÁ JEDNOTKA* (best in unit). Border guards retained the above mentioned badge, except latter versions were made of painted aluminium.

The People's Militia (LM) received an award similar to the generic armed forces excellence badge previously described with the difference that the centre featured a militia man wearing a beret and the legend: *VZORNY MILICIONAR* on a blue ribbon. The base was decorated with the initial letters LM. All of these badges were issued with screw back attachments.

(**Above**) CSSR Czechoslovakian People's Army type two generic Excellent Soldier Badges in brass and enamel with white ribbon. The type one was the service-specific excellence badge and the type two was in fact the first of the generic-type badges. The type three had a blue ribbon and the type four was painted aluminium.

(**Above**) CSSR Czechoslovakian People's Army type four Excellent Soldier; Border Guard; Militia.

(**Above**) A group of Czechoslovakian conscripts photographed in the 1950s. They wear a variety of field caps decorated with the subdued insignia of that era. The man third from left wears one of the trade specific excellence badges. A like photograph of Soviet soldiers would have shown all the men wearing at least one award of some description and it amply demonstrates the comparative rarity of many Czechoslovakian awards.

(**Above**) CSSR Czechoslovakian People's Army Best in Unit.

Proficiency Badges

USSR

In addition to excellence badges, the Soviet conscript and career NCO could also qualify for the Military Proficiency Badge, which recognized technical excellence and professional competency over four grades: master, one, two and three. Issued in the 1950s through to 1991, the original type was made of good quality brass and enamel with a screw attachment to the rear. The design featured a brass shield within which was a field of blue (armed forces) or green (border guards) containing either a white Cyrillic M or white Arabic numeral. The top of the badge was crowned by a red-enamelled Soviet star flanked by sprigs of laurel, while the base was decorated with a laurel wreath. The blue field was punctuated by lots of little stars in order to give the enamel a textured finish. It was made by a variety of manufacturers, all of whom used their own moulds, creating slight variations in the shape and size of the shield. Between 1968 and c.1975, a slightly cheaper version was issued, replacing the enamel details with plastic and the screw attachment with a pin. Of interest, the stars were removed from the blue field. These badges were replaced in the 1970s by a final version made using painted aluminium. On this type the stars returned to the blue field, the paint upon which is often so dark that it appears to be black, but is in fact still blue. The gilt paint came in a variety of shades ranging from silver-gilt to antique gold. Most commonly, these badges had a pin, but some did see a return to the screw. Often the border is painted white, although it is not clear whether this was an official measure or not. The Russian Federation did continue the use of this badge, in a modified form, with a screw and white-painted border. Military fashion often precedes military doctrine, so an improvised fashion could have become formally adopted. It is a matter for discussion. As can be expected, the earlier brass version is the rarest, although the master class in all types is noticeably scarcer than its contemporaries. Between those issued by the armed forces and the border guards, the Border Guard Proficiency Badge is significantly rarer than its blue counterpart. Any example of this type, therefore, should be regarded as a lucky find.

(**Left**) USSR Soviet Armed Forces Proficiency and Sports Badges (top): 1960s brass and enamel Master Class Military Proficiency; painted aluminium other ranks tropical cap badge, larger than the standard M41; 1970s brass and enamel-effect plastic coated Master Class Proficiency; (second): 1960s brass and enamel Military Proficiency classes one, two, and three; (third): c.1966–94 Military Sports class first, second, third; (bottom): 1970s–91 painted aluminium Proficiency Badges class one, two, and three.

(**Above right**) USSR Soviet Armed Forces 1970s–91 painted aluminium Military Proficiency Badge with additional painted border.

(**Below**) USSR Soviet Armed Forces Military Proficiency Badges 1970s painted aluminium with paler blue backgrounder and 1970s enamel-effect plastic master class. The two badges together clearly demonstrate the difference between the version with stars to the blue field and the version without.

(Left) Soviet NCO photographed c.1966 wearing the Army Excellence Badge alongside the Army Proficiency Badge and two sports badges, the closest of which is the 1966-type Army Sports Badge.

Romania

(Above) RPR and RSR Romanian People's Army (top): Air Mechanic Proficiency grade one; Excellent Infantry; Excellent Soldier; Excellent Tanker; Air Mechanic grade two; (middle): RSR Signals Proficiency grade two; Tank Proficiency grade two; RPR Signals Proficiency; Tank Proficiency grade three; RSR Signals Proficiency grade three; (bottom): Pilot Proficiency; Generic Army Excellence.

Bulgaria

Bulgaria copied the tradition of proficiency badges and produced its own range between the 1950s and 1980s. These Bulgarian examples were quite similar, except they had a squarer shape with a plain, white, enamelled field (with number) and red banner containing the initials: BNA. They do not appear as often as their Soviet counterparts and so command a comparatively higher price, although they are not rare as far as Bulgarian badges go.

Romania preferred a more individual approach to its proficiency badges and so produced a range of badges relevant to specific skills, rather than one for general proficiency. These included number-graded badges (usually ranged from one down to three) for signals, armoured crews, mountain troops, sappers and divers (which had a forth class). Many of these were produced by the RPR and RSR, although the RPR did make a greater use of clasps than the RSR, so not all badges were of the same type. As such, and as a consequence of their increased age, the RPR versions are much rarer. In most cases, the main difference was the state coat-of-arms, otherwise both regimes made the badges of enamelled or painted brass. Those for signals, armoured crews and mountain troops appear to be the most common (especially grades two and three). The Romanian Air Force favoured white metal eagles with the state coat-of-arms attached to its chest. In its talons it clutched a number of devices according to the branch-of-service: georgette (pilots and paratroops), bomb (navigator), cogwheel (air mechanic), disc with lightening rods (signals), cogwheel and lightening (communication engineer), and so on – all of which were graded from one through to unclassified.

(Above) Bulgarian People's Arm and USSR Soviet Armed Forces Military Proficiency Badges. The Bulgarian People's Army was the only non-Soviet member state to follow the Soviet lead. Most other Pact nations employed their own pattern badges or clasps. The Soviet badge is of the comparatively rare enamel-effect plastic variety.

(Left) RSR Romanian People's Army Sapper grade two.

(Below) RSR Romanian People's Army Air Force Proficiency Badges (left to right): Navigator; Parachute Qualification; Air Technician.

Hungary

Hungary favoured clasps more, but it did still produce at least one proficiency badge. This was for signalmen and is said to have been issued in the 1950s, which seems most likely as the signals clasp was issued from the 1960s onwards. The badge had a large oval wreath crowned by a red star. The centre had a white field within which was a brass signals branch-of-service badge. The base of the wreath had a separate brass plate upon which was recorded the grade: one, two or three. Curved with a pin back it was quite a substantial badge by Hungarian standards and was issued in enamels or a combination of paint and enamel-effect plastic.

(Right) Hungarian People's Army (top): Excellent Squad Leader first award; Excellent Border Guard; Excellent Squad Leader second award; (second): Excellent Militia; Excellent Militia enamel version; Worker's Militia Excellent Leader; (third): Military Academy later type; Police; Police Graduation; (bottom): Signals Proficiency class one, two and three. The class two is of a cheaper painted type rather than enamel.

(Below) CSSR Czechoslovakian Border Guard (top) proficiency grades one and two (bottom) Excellent Dog Handler, Honoured Helper.

30

Airborne Badges

USSR

The first Soviet badge to fall within the realms of this study is the Paratrooper Qualification Badge, issued between 1955 and 1968. It replaced the more modestly designed 1936 type and was an item the food-conscious Hungarians referred to as the 'ice cream cone'. Its basic design was a cone-shaped parachute featuring a Soviet star and an aeroplane in flight made of an impressed brass and enamel. The aeroplane could be an integral part of the badge or come as a separate piece attached by a central pin. Distinctive from the replacement 1968-type, it had an aeroplane that was slightly fatter, with the body tilted at a higher angle and the engines positioned closer to the body. The Advanced Parachute Badge, which recorded multiple jumps, had loops fitted to the base to which a number hanger was attached. The range of numbers varied, but tended to climb in multiples of ten and fifteen, with most being double-sided for a quick exchange. Three possible shapes existed: heart, georgette and shield – the latter being found most commonly on the 1968-type Instructor Badge. Early examples can be recognized by the shape of the numbers as the earlier hangers tended to have angular numbers and the 1968-type more rounded. As with the more common 1968-type it had the legend: *Advanced Parachutist* featured on the canopy.

(**Above left**) USSR Soviet Armed Forces 1936-type Parachute Qualification. Miniature civilian lapel badge made from painted aluminium.

(**Above right**) USSR Soviet Armed Forces 1955-type Parachute Qualification Badges (left to right): two-piece Advanced Parachute with number hanger; two-piece Basic Parachute; one-piece Advanced Parachute with number hanger.

(**Left**) Two Soviet NCO paratroopers in 1955 wearing the 1950s-pattern sports badges and the early pattern Komsomol youth pin. The man on the right wears the 1936-type Parachute Badge, which was replaced that same year by the new generation of parachute badges featured in this book.

31

(**Above**) USSR Soviet Armed Forces 1968 Basic Parachute Qualification Badges (left to right): early example with old style aeroplane; later type with new, slimmer aeroplane.

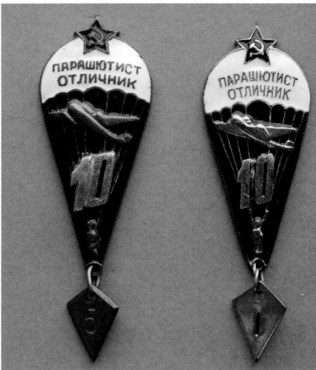

(**Above**) USSR Soviet Armed Forces 1968 Advanced Parachute Qualification Badges (left to right): early type; later type with smaller aeroplane, lettering, and number ten.

Both of the above were replaced in 1968 by an extended family of badges. The basic qualification badge remained much the same, except it had a hole at its base in order to accommodate a diamond-shaped number hanger. In most cases double-sided, the number diamond started at one and went through to nine. The aeroplanes on the earlier examples were still a little on the fat side, but became slimmer during the course of the 1970s. When ten or more jumps had been recorded, the paratrooper qualified for the Advanced Parachute Badge. This was distinguished by a Cyrillic legend upon the canopy and a large, gilt ten in the centre of the badge for the first award. At its base was attached the same diamond-shaped hanger previously described to record the jumps between eleven and nineteen.

As a general rule, the parachute qualification badges were of good-quality brass and enamels, although the complexity of the manufacture was subject to alterations as the 1980s wore on. The two latter examples featured a narrower body. one was decorated with an enamelled paint, while the other had a smooth finish on the reverse as opposed to the customary mirror image. Diamond number pendants can be encountered in raw aluminium, although this is rare. Most of the number diamonds remained a good-quality brass distinguishable from the post-Soviet versions by virtue of the fact that the originals are roughly twice the thickness. The only Advanced Parachute Badges that seem consistently to be of a lower quality are those numbered between twenty and ninety-nine jumps. These numbered badges are unusually scarce when compared to their surrounding counterparts and have most frequently been encountered as cheaper painted aluminium. Possibly, once the nineteen mile-stone was reached, a paratrooper progressed swiftly through to the early 100s and so would not

have worn a twenty through to ninety-nine badge for very long. As something of a go-between towards instructor status, a better quality badge may not have been thought necessary. Even so, it still does not account for their comparative rarity when it is considered how common are the badges that record jumps of several hundred. It is interesting to think where these badges, once eclipsed by a higher award, went to? One explanation could come from the fact that cloth versions of this badge have been encountered, although close inspection has never been possible, so they may yet prove to be fantasy pieces.

The 1968-type Instructor Badge was significantly larger than the other examples previously described. Its increased size was to accommodate both the inscription on the canopy and the 100 multiples attached to the body. As with the Advanced Parachute Badge, the number was a separate piece, but, unlike the former, the aeroplane was also separately attached on the early to mid versions. In both cases the number and aeroplane on the earlier 1968-type badge differs from the later types issued from the mid-1970s. The main numbers ranged from 100 to 1000, with additional jumps recorded on a two-ring number hanger. Most frequently, these number hangers increased in units of fifteen (the most common of which was the ten to twenty-five hangers to the obverse and reverse sides), although hangers with consecutive numbers did exist for the earlier type. In manufacturing terms, the 1968-type Instructor Badge can be divided into three ages: early, middle and later. The earlier type had the fatter aeroplane and bolder lettering, when compared to that of the later types. The middle type had the slimmer aeroplane and lettering, but did retain the three-piece construction, whereas the later type was a one-piece stamping, which gave it a noticeably flatter appear-

(Clockwise from top left) USSR Soviet Armed Forces 1968-type Advanced Parachute Qualification badge with forty jumps. This example is of the cheaper painted aluminium variety. Both its number and its materials of manufacture make it quite scarce in comparison to the enamelled type.

USSR Soviet Armed Forces 1968-type Advanced Parachute Qualification with twenty-one jumps. This type is of a very late painted version not commonly encountered.

USSR Soviet Armed Forces 1969 Parachute Instructor Qualification Badges (left to right): old version with large size aeroplane; later type with slimmer aeroplane. Both are three-piece constructions with a separate aeroplane attached by pins.

USSR Soviet Armed Forces 1968 Parachute Instructor Qualification Badge. Late single-piece construction with painted rather than the more usual enamelled decoration.

USSR Soviet Armed Forces 1968 type Parachute Instructor Qualification Badge. Late type with painted details, but unusually two-piece construction with separate number.

ance. The later type also observed a further economy in that the number hanger was made of painted aluminium and some examples had a painted body, rather than enamelled details. A final type of this class was different to all the rest in that it was solid. The example featured has no maker's mark so little else can be said except that it was coloured by translucent enamel paint.

During the 1970s and 1980s Soviet parachute instructors could also have qualified for a graded instructor badge. Almost identical to the 1968-type, at a glance, it did still have a number of noticeable differences, chiefly the absence of any numerals and number hanger. Instead, the badge had a horizontal band across its centre with the award grade: I, II or III. The background colour varied with the first-class blue and the second-class blue-green. The final and most significant difference was the quality of construction, which (being made of a solid cast lightweight painted aluminium) was much cheaper, the thickness of which varied. Any perceived lack of quality, however, should not dissuade the serious collector, as this award is considerably rarer than the 1968-type Parachute Instructor Badge.

Hungary

Hungarian paratroopers could qualify for a circular badge, which featured a descending parachute contained within a laurel wreath crowned by a red star. As with very many Hungarian badges, this example had the opposing finger attachments to the rear, but also had additional twin claws at its base. Unusually, the better quality examples made of brass and enamel were of a later issue (of which there are two variants: pale blue or dark blue backgrounds). Those of an earlier issue (1970s) were painted. The enamelled version survived the change of regime in 1989 and a post-communist version without star can occasionally be encountered. In addition to the painted and enamelled versions described, a wire-embroidered badge was also available for offi-

cers. This was stitched on black felt with a cloth backing and of very good quality, although, in keeping with the fragile nature of wire embroidery, few have survived in good condition. Instructors wore a similar badge with an additional scroll to the base which read: OKTATO. The number of jumps was recorded on a separate badge called the Master Jumper Badge. The design was a wreathed light-bulb shape with a descending parachute within its centre, upon which was superimposed an aeroplane in flight and the relevant number of jumps. The badge was made of brass and lacquered to give it an enamelled effect. Across its base was the Hungarian flag and the legend: Mesterugro. Paratroopers could also qualify for a graded sky-diving clasp and the standard conscript's proficiency bar (see clasps).

(Above) Hungarian People's Army Standard Parachute Qualification Badge. Early type with paint and enamel lacquered details.

(Above) Hungarian People's Army Standard Parachute Qualification Badge. Later 1980s-type with pale blue field. The post-communist era parachute badges of this type also have a pale blue field and so this badge most probably represents the last of the HPA examples.

(**Above**) Hungarian People's Army Standard Parachute Qualification Badges (left to right): 1980s enamelled version with dark blue field; officer's wire embroidered.

(**Above**) Hungarian People's Army (left to right): Master Jumper, 250 award; 1970s Parachute Instructor Qualification Badge; Master Jumper, 500 award. Higher awards had a separate number plate applied.

CSSR

Prior to 1968 Czechoslovakia had maintained a parachute brigade, but after the Soviet invasion, the size of its parachute force was reduced to that of a regiment, containing four battalions: active, reserve, special operations and training personnel. Those who served in the 22nd Brigade and beyond had the opportunity to qualify for the Parachute Proficiency Badge, which came in six sequential grades: basic, third, second, first class, master and instructor. The frequently suggested date of issue is 1965, although this is not absolutely certain. They all featured the same basic design, a descending parachute with a red star at its base and Art Deco-style wings to the sides. The identifying feature was to be found in the centre of the badge: golden aeroplane in flight signified the basic qualification; classes one to three featured number shields; while the master and instructor badges were decorated with inscribed scrolls: *MISTR* and *INSTRUKTOR*. The lettering was either highlighted with red paint of left plain. All grades had a screw back with locking nut and plastic washer. The badges illustrating this book are the lightweight painted aluminium examples issued in the 1970s and 1980s.

(**Above**) CSSR Parachute Qualification Badges (left to right): Instructor, alternative type without red lettering; basic issue; second class, third class – notice the difference in colour and quality.

(**Right**) CSSR Parachute Instructor Qualification Badge with red lettering.

Soviet Guards Badges

The first Guards Badge was issued in 1943 and was generally worn on the area around the wearer's right breast (period photographs demonstrate no specific location), but during the Cold War, the placement of the badge became more prescribed.

With the exception of combat decorations, the Guards Badge took precedence over other badges and was placed closest to the second button down from the collar on the M69 field and service tunics. Often the same order of wear was observed on the parade tunic, although an alternative arrangement was also encountered where the Guards Badge was placed above all other standard awards.

Of all the badges surveyed within this study, this was unique to the USSR. (Other Pact nations preferred their own military distinctions with which to identify their elite formations, e.g. the NVA wore a variety of cuff titles.) For a comparative study of

Soviet Major photographed in 1951 wearing one of the wartime Guards Badges.

(**Above**) USSR Soviet Armed Forces World War II issue Guards Badge in enamel and gilt-finished brass. The most distinctive feature of the Wartime issue badges is their lack of a tasselled fringe to the bottom of the banner.

Soviet NCO from 1964 wearing a selection of badges with the Guards Badge arranged in an alternative to the more commonly prescribed order of wear. In addition to the Guards Badge he also wears an Army Excellence Badge and two sports badges, the latter of which is the non-military GTO Sports Badge. His peaked cap displays the M41 pattern insignia.

(**Right**) USSR Soviet Armed Forces Guards Badges (left to right): World War II issue; 1980s issue with circular shaped wreath; unusual alloy version.

Grad
attractive
1961 and
field with
(towards
Overall, it
attached b
gilt finish,
ment to the
duced in
coat-of-arr
enamel sta

Highe
1950. They
nical colleg
name-plate
across the
1954. These
parts attach
1954 and 1
were attache
unified vers
name plate
attached by
Russian silv
made of the
most moder
doctors or e
and graduate
their civilian
possible bec
graduation b
equivalent of

Other v
copies bough
place of the o
emy name-pl
the officer an
They can eas
The star and
and well-deta
mark was als
rivets and no
badges have a
The reverse l
genuine Sovie
have a mark, it
be aware that
general mark c
which should a
of a sturdy an
unheard of for
their uniform,
reserved their
wear on their
jeweller's copi
conforming to
form to a high s
tographic or do

USSR
order c

has n
Wire
head-
NCOs
felt, b
to the
no cor
lar my
found
unhea
made
Navy
in the
World
tions.
not ag
cause
appea
been

Guards Badges the reader would have to visit Cuba, as it was this socialist state whose badges most closely copied the awards of the USSR, largely because the Cuban badges were manufactured in the USSR. The Guards Badge was also unusual in that it was the only badge to fulfil the dual roles of award and insignia. It rewarded the conscript for having survived the rigours of their training (fatalities, although infrequent, did occur and were an accepted risk – especially for those serving in airborne units). In addition, it served to identify the elite status of his unit and commemorate its past courage with the assumption he would maintain and perpetuate the honour of the division (which he would have had ample opportunity to do as the guards regiments were always placed at the forefront of any attack).

The actual Guards Badge itself changed very little between 1943 and 1991. The majority of the observable differences were to be found in the quality of the materials used and the methods of construction, the greatest degree of variation occurring in the late 1960s and 1970s. For the most part, probably because of its elite status, the Guards Badge was of good quality gilt-finished brass and enamel, heavily stamped with a mirror image to the reverse and screw attachment. The basic design was a laurel wreath enclosing a red star on a white field. Above it was a red banner containing the Cyrillic legend for the word 'guard'. A brass plate at the base recorded the state initials: *CCCP*. Those manufactured during and just after World War II had a fuller wreath, while all later examples were somewhat flatter in appearance. The shape of the wreath also

USSR Soviet Armed Forces generic excellence badges and Guards Badges (top): Army, Navy, Air Force Excellence – 1970s–91 painted aluminium; (bottom): economy painted aluminium Guards Badge; late-issue painted aluminium; 1960s-issue painted aluminium – note this example has a more silver colour, possibly due to the gilt paint having been absorbed by the metal over time.

badge was a gilt wreath of oak and laurel leaves tied with a ribbon. The reverse featured the standard pin-and-clasp attachment common to Romanian badges. Those of the RPR featured the early type state coat-of-arms, whereas the RSR used their own version. Generals qualified for a slightly different graduation badge, which followed roughly the same criteria as before mentioned, except it was fractionally larger, had an enamelled red star behind the coat-of-arms, and carried the legend: *ACADEMIA MILITARA GENERALA*. The reverse detail was different in that it was individually numbered. Military schools issued badges that featured a gilt wreath, central motif relevant to its particular area of expertise and a descriptive legend. The example featured is that from a flight school.

(Right) A group of Romanian officers alongside Army General Zinea (centre) photographed in 1978. Both Zinea and the first man on the left wear the RSR Graduation Badges.

(Above) RSR Pilot Officer Training School Graduation Badge.

(Above) RPR Defence of the Motherland Association Instructor Training School Graduation Badge.

(Right) US...

Qualificatio...

Poland

Surprisingly, when compared to what would normally be expected of Poland, graduation badges awarded by the Polish People's Army were strikingly similar to those of the USSR; the main differences, however, were to be found in the choice of language and insignia. The Polish graduation badge featured a squared enamel shield with a red field upon which was mounted a silver eagle (state eagle and not the military eagle found on cap insignia). Below was a silver ribbon that recorded the individual academy's initials. Overall, they were a four-piece construction with a screw attachment. All metal parts were made of silver and attached to the body of the badge by wire pins. Military schools offered a more modest, but no less attractive, badge; these had a smooth-bordered diamond with a ruby-coloured enamel field. The silver name-ribbon was an integral part of the badge, as was the eagle during the 1950s and 1960s. During the 1970s the design was altered slightly when the eagle became a separate piece, of a type identical to that used on the higher graduation badges.

(Above) Poland. 1950s-type Military Training School Graduation Badge. Note how the eagle is an integral part of the badge. Later examples had the eagle mounted as a separate piece.

(Below) Poland (left to right): Officer Higher Training Academy Graduation badges; Military Training School Graduation Badges.

Bulgaria

The Bulgarian People's Army, in keeping with its cultural affinities with the Soviet Union, followed the traditional design of officer graduate badges very closely. The only key difference between those of Soviet and Bulgarian manufacture was that the Bulgarian badges featured the Bulgarian state emblem (rampant lion in a silver wreath mounted by a star) in place of the USSR coat-of-arms. The reverse differed in that the Bulgarian badges had a hollow body rather than a solid back, possibly a reflection of its poorer economy. Early examples were made of silver and hot enamel, although later versions used lacquered or plastic enamel that has since discoloured a creamy brown colour.

Military schools did not follow the same traditions as the USSR and so established their own characteristic design, which was a gilt laurel wreath within which was contained the relevant branch-of-service insignia. At the top, where the two points of the wreath met, the Bulgarian lion was contained within a brass disc, except for reserve officer schools. For these establishments, probably because they catered for more than one branch of service, the lion was centrally placed at the expense of the customary branch-of-service insignia. Quality varies, but the coloured detail was most often rendered in enamel paint rather than hot enamel. In some cases only the national colours were applied and the remainder was left plain.

(**Above**) Bulgarian People's Army Training School Graduation badge for a reserve officer.

(**Above**) Bulgarian people's Army Officer Higher Academy Graduation Badge.

CSSR

The design of the first Czechoslovakian graduation badges followed that of the Soviet type, the only difference being that the Czech version featured the 1950s pattern Czech lion within a red star rather than the USSR coat-of-arms. After 1960 the graduation badges adopted the same pentagonal device common to cap insignia of the 1960 to 1989 era. The pentagonal device was a part of the main body on the enamelled versions with a separate lion attached by a single rivet, whereas later, painted examples were of a single construction. In keeping with many lacquered badges, the later graduation badges have since discoloured and, in many cases, started to become detached from the surface of the badge. In the future, although already quite a scarce badge now, examples able to have survived in good condition will be exceptionally rare. The reverse was attached to the tunic by the customary screw and plate. Military schools awarded an oval wreath with the state emblem as its centre piece and a white enamelled ribbon below to record the relevant legend.

(**Right**) CSSR Czechoslovakian People's Army Officer Higher Academy Graduation Badge. Late version made from a single piece construction painted and lacquered.

Sports Badges

USSR

The Soviet Army employed a simple set of sports badges that came in three grades: I, II, III. The first version to mention was instituted in the 1940s and was used up until c.1955. Two basic types existed: one with the grade and corresponding two-letter initials, and a second with just the number. Other than that, and a slight difference in size, the design was near identical. The badge featured an enamelled banner containing the initials: *CCCP*, below which was a cogwheel that contained a white field and red star and a man running through a broken finishing line (inscribed with minute letters) beneath which was a white shield containing the relevant grade flanked by laurel leaves. The reverse had an imprint of the obverse detail and was attached via a screw and plate. In spite of their age, and unlike other awards of the same era, these sports badges are not particularly rare and so are still cheap to buy.

The above badges were replaced c.1955 by a second range of sports badges, which again were graded I, II, III. In addition, they were also colour-coded red, blue and green. Variations included two- and one-piece constructions, differences in the size of the star or the runner contained within it, and stars with pebbled fields as opposed to lines. Made of brass and enamel, the top half featured a wreath with red hammer and sickle. The bottom half was decorated by a coloured inscription: red (first), blue (second), green (third). The centre had a white field upon which was a cogwheel, over which was placed a red star with a man running through a finishing tape. (Interestingly, he ran in an opposite direction to the man on the 1940s pattern.) The reverse was either attached by a screw or a pin, of which the pin is the rarer of the two. They remained in issue until 1965/66. In spite of this brief period, though, they are not to be considered as being particularly rare – scarce at the very most.

(**Left**) USSR Soviet Armed Forces 1940s to mid-1950s military sports badges. Notice slight variations in the design.

(**Below**) USSR Soviet Armed Forces 1950s-mid-1960s Military Sports Badges (left to right): first, second, third classes.

In 1966 a third and final type of this class badge was introduced. This design featured a small, painted aluminium star within which was contained a red, blue or green field surrounded by a white border. The coloured field featured a runner, while the white border contained the descriptive legend, which in the case of this badge was the same for each class; beneath that was a small, coloured field within which was contained the badge's grade. They remained in service until after the end of the USSR and were not discontinued until 1994. They came in a variety of types due to differences in manufacturer. The colour of the gilt paint can range from antique gold through to an almost silver shade. Some were shallow cast with a screw, while others were solid with a simple pin. They are not at all rare in their first- and second-class grades, although it is interesting to note that the third class is scarce and not as frequently encountered.

Other sports badges existed, the most common of which was a simple competition badge, introduced during the early 1960s; in rare cases enamelled, but more commonly painted aluminium. It came in four grades: I (red), II (blue), III (green) and IV (yellow). The grade was contained within a small, coloured field at the top of the badge, flanked by laurel leaves, below which was a white band containing the Cyrillic legend for the word 'sport'. Below that was a coloured field within which was contained a silver runner. Slightly rarer were small, square competition badges that could (below a generic master class) range from any sporting event between chess and parachuting. The design featured the Soviet flag at the top with a band of laurel leaves below. Beneath the leaves was a picture of the sporting event and the award's grade: I, II or III. Constructed from two-pieces of painted aluminium, they were a simple yet attractive badge, but due to their comparative rarity, and the fact that some are associated with paratroops, they can still command a reasonable level of interest.

(Clockwise from above)

USSR Soviet Armed Forces sports badges (top): various sport specific awards (bottom) generic sports badge; (left to right): original brass and enamelled type; later painted aluminium. Both third class.

USSR Soviet Armed Forces Military Parachute Sports Badge, third class. Some versions of this badge had a hole at the bottom in order to accommodate an additional diamond-shaped number hanger.

USSR civilian youth sports association. Awards such as these, although civilian in nature, were frequently featured on the uniforms of military conscripts.

Hungary

The Hungarian People's Army took its sports quite seriously and frequently organized events for its troops. A variety of awards was available to the successful participants, the most commonly encountered of which was the KHT and then later KTP sports badges. The first type was the KHT (army gymnastics) featuring two crossed scimitars with a star and state coat-of-arms mounted upon them. At its base was a scroll containing the initials: KHT. Awarded from the late 1950s to mid-1960s, in five grades, it was issued in gold with wreath, gold, silver, bronze and iron. As can be expected, the iron class was the most common. As a collective, though, when compared to the later KTP sports badge, all of these earlier examples are comparatively scarce.

Issued between the mid-1960s up until 1989, the KTP (army athletics) sports badge was – at a glance – identical to the KHT awards except for two small points: the scroll contained the new initials, KTP, while the state coat-of-arms was of a modified design (the lines and detail of the KHT was more clearly defined). Within the KTP family of badges there were also differences between the state coat-of-arms in that some had a red star with clear gloss and others matt paint.

In addition to the KTP and KHT badges there existed also the Unit Championship Competition Badge (*EGYSÉG BAJNOKSÁG*). These were a two-piece construction featuring a wreathed shield upon which was attached a small football. The ball came in both bronze and silver, but this difference was more a matter of age or manufacturer than class distinction. Class was determined by the colour of the wreath: gold, silver and bronze. However, this can now be difficult to determine as the protective lacquer applied at the time of manufacture has frequently discoloured. In all grades, this badge should be considered as the most common of all the Hungarian sports badges. Of a slightly rarer type was the near identical Training Championship Competition Badge, distinguished by the alternative legend: *TANITEZETI BAJNOKSÁG*. Both of these badges were attached to the uniform by the characteristic opposing fingers.

Bulgaria

The Bulgarian People's Army broke with tradition from the Soviet Army when it came to the design of its sports badges. It came in three grades: first, second and third. Typical of very many Bulgarian badges, the national flag was a prominent feature of the design below which a running soldier was contained within a red star. Beneath the soldier was a coloured field containing the relevant Roman numeral, below which was a white semi-circle featuring a Cyrillic legend. Unlike the majority of Soviet sports badges, the Bulgarian version was not distinguished by any colour, so a keen eye is required in order to tell them apart.

DDR

The NVA's main sports award was the *NVA Militärsportsabzeichen* (Military Sports Badge). It featured a gilt oak wreath with a rifle in its open centre, from which few a flag with the initials: NVA. The badge was issued between the years 1969 and 1990 and so was one of the NVA's most common awards. However, due to the use of a ferrous metal within its construction, it has since become quite scarce to find a Military Sports Badge in good condition. Nearly all surviving examples have invariably started to rust and, in future years, a good-condition badge of this type will have become quite a rare thing. It would pay a collector to take good care of the one they have now.

(Right) Hungarian People's Army Military Sports Award. Early post-1957 type. Large gilt and enamel award. The red star would originally have had a brass state coat-of-arms superimposed upon it.

(Right) Hungarian People's Army Master Sergeant Balogh photographed in the 1960s wearing the silver class KHT Sports Badge. (Kind permission of Mrs Balogh.)

(Right) Hungarian People's Army KHT Sports Badge in bronze. This award preceded the more commonly encountered KTP family of sports badges and is often of slightly superior quality.

(Right) DDR National People's Army Sports Badge in gold.

el. The reverse was shallow stamped with a pin-and-clasp attachment. The pendant, which was double-sided, recorded the number of additional years' service in single units. Of this first type, two basic variations existed: those with a slim wreath and bold star, and those with a fuller wreath but less pronounced star (these differences reflected changes in manufacturer). Later examples, from the early 1970s to 1991, were made of painted aluminium, but in all other respects remained the same. As far as availability goes, little difference stands between those of brass manufacture and painted aluminium, whereas there is a noticeable variation between the services, with the navy clasp significantly rarer than its counterparts.

The air force produced the greatest range of clasps within the Soviet Armed Forces. The two most commonly encountered types were for pilots and navigators, the design of which was very similar to one another throughout most of this period. In its basic form, it featured a brass-edged blue shield within which was contained the relevant grade. Stylized wings extended from the shield, which itself was crowned by a red enamel star. The 1950 to 1961 type pilot clasp matched this description with a screw attachment to the rear and crossed swords behind the shield. The 1950 to 1961 navigator badge featured a brass bomb with engraved red number and wings extending outward from the centre. The third class had a blue, painted bomb, but was otherwise the same. Hungarian versions were almost identical except they had a pin attachment to the reverse and the third class featured an enamelled panel within which the number three was contained. Details of what happened between 1961 and 1965 are vague but the design of the pilot and navigator badges may

well have adopted a more modest design. The two contenders featured a clasp with crossed swords and a central red star for pilots, and a bomb with mounted red star for navigators; but they could have as likely come from the 1940s as they do resemble the air technical clasp of that era. In 1966 a final version was produced. Its design matched the 1950-type except the crossed swords were longer, a pin and clasp was applied to the rear, and the first and second classes had silver wreaths surrounding the shield. In 1971 a sniper class was added, which featured an aircraft on a blue field with a written description below on red enamel and naturalistic wings. NCOs are said to have qualified for an unclassified award that featured a numberless shield. Unlike the other clasps, which remained of good quality up until the end, this clasp is found in painted aluminium, as well as brass and enamels. Between c.1988 and 1991 a final clasp was produced, a generic pilot clasp featuring a near identical design to that of the sniper class with the following differences: it was made from painted aluminium, had a screw back and replaced the written inscription with the initials, *BBC*.

Fight engineers between 1948 and 1958 could qualify for a non-rated clasp made of silver-plated brass, a shallow stamping with a pin-and-clasp attachment. It featured a central red star behind which was a crossed hammer and wrench, from which extended narrow wings. Between 1950 and 1961 a rated version was produced. It had much the same appearance as the pilot clasp except the crossed swords were replaced by a hammer and wrench behind a shield with a green field. This was replaced by a return of the non-rated clasp, which was made from painted aluminium.

(Above) USSR Soviet Armed Forces (top to bottom): Unclassified Air Technician; 1955–61-type Navigator first class.

(Right) USSR Soviet Armed Forces (top to bottom): 1971 Pilots Proficiency Clasp 'sniper' class; 1966-type Pilot Proficiency Clasps first, second and third classes.

(Far right) USSR Soviet Armed Forces (top to bottom): 1966-type Navigator Clasps classes first, second and third; Unclassified Pilots Proficiency Clasp.

(**Above**) USSR Soviet Armed Forces (top to bottom): Naval Pilot Clasp; 1950s Signals Proficiency Clasp second class; late-issue Soviet Air Force Pilots Proficiency Clasp.

(**Above**) USSR Soviet Armed Forces (top to bottom): Soviet Commander Submarine Clasps in gold and silver; Soviet Commander Clasp for surface craft.

Marine officer pilots flying aircraft carrier-based aeroplanes had their own clasp. It featured a red star superimposed on an anchor behind which was a pair of extended wings. Issued from c.1948 to the end of the Cold War it is an interesting, but not uncommon or valuable clasp. It is uncertain, but it may well have been graded gold, silver and bronze, as silver and bronze examples have been encountered.

The Soviet Navy rewarded its seaborne officers with one of two clasps: submarine and surface vessels. In two classes they came in gold and silver. The submarine featured the side profile of a World War II class submarine with a red star in its centre (which sometimes contained a hammer and sickle), while the surface vessel featured a small to medium-sized ship with a screw attachment. Other Pact nations with a navy followed this pattern and adapted the design to meet their own traditions – largely swapping the red star for a national flag (Bulgaria, DDR and Romania) or national emblem (Poland).

Bulgaria

Bulgaria followed the USSR's lead quiet closely and produced a combined services' clasp identical in all but a few details. The key differences were the BNA's use of silver rather than gold, the inclusion of the armed forces' initials and the use of painted aluminium more than enamelled brass. Air force badges were only fractionally different from those of the USSR. The pilot and navigator clasps featured a red field and had a rampant lion as the centre piece of the master/sniper class. Air technicians had a clasp with a green field. The only original clasp was that issued to parachutists and was graded from one down to three and then unclassified. It featured a central descending parachute backed by crossed swords with outstretched brass wings. Early examples were made from brass and enamel with later versions made from painted brass and then painted aluminium. In all cases they were attached with a screw and plate.

(**Above**) USSR Soviet Armed Forces (top to bottom): Soviet Armoured Crewman Proficiency Clasp third class; Bulgarian People's Army Combined Services Proficiency Clasp first class; 1966–90-type DDR Border Guard Dog Handler Proficiency Clasp.

(**Above**) Bulgarian People's Army (top to bottom): Pilot Proficiency Clasp 'sniper' class; Unclassified Parachute Proficiency Clasp.

(**Above**) Poland and CSSR Czechoslovakian People's Army (top to bottom): Poland Armoured Crewman Proficiency Clasp; CSSR General Proficiency Clasp master class.

Poland

Poland did not appear to show particularly great enthusiasm for clasps. Research has only found a clasp issued to armoured crewmen; the same in principle to the Soviet version except the red star was replaced by an enamelled, white eagle. No other clasps, other than those described for the navy above, have come to light.

CSSR

Czechoslovakia seemed as little interested in clasps as Poland. It awarded only one clasp of note the General Service Clasp. This clasp had a central, white field surrounded by a silver wreath. The white field contained the clasp's grade: M (master), one, two or three. Extending from the wreath was a pair of stylized silver wings. Early examples were made of brass and white metal while the latter examples were made of painted aluminium – attached to the tunic by small claws. A rarer alternative pattern existed with a small, numbered rectangle from which extended a spray of laurel leaves.

(**Above**) CSSR Czechoslovakian People's Army (top): early issue army cap badge; general proficiency clasp first class; 1970s–89 Worker's Militia cap badge; (second): general proficiency clasp second class; late-issue Officer Higher Training Academy Graduation Badge; general proficiency clasp third class; (middle): various cap badges with additional painted aluminium surrounds; (forth): Parachute Qualification Badges: instructor, basic, second class, third class; (bottom): Excellent Soldier Badges: army and air force; border guard; worker's militia.

(**Above**) Poland. Armoured Crewman Proficiency Clasp third class.

Hungary

Alongside the DDR, Hungary most enthusiastically embraced the use of qualification clasps. Little existed prior to the 1960s, with the only example having been found being a Soviet-styled clasp for armoured vehicles, shallow stamped with a basic pin attachment and numbered one to three.

By 1965 a wide variety of clasps ranged from class one down to three had come into existence. They were widely available and covered not just the standard branch-of-service trades, such as infantry, paratroops or armour, but also some of the more specialized skills, such as bomb disposal. Made of a heavyweight brass the obverse featured a blue field (which varied in shade from dark to pale) decorated with gilt and painted Hungarian People's Army flag on its left side, beneath which was attached a separate brass number shield. The right-hand arm featured the individual qualification's identifying motif. The reverse was fitted with a claw plate. Early examples had a slightly domed plastic coating to the obverse, while the later examples were lacquered. In all cases they do not survive particularly well, especially the claws which very often snap with repeat bending.

In addition to the parachute clasp, a skydiving clasp also existed. It featured a parachute and picture of a skydiver as its centre piece surrounded by a narrow wreath. The base of the wreath held a small shield upon which was recorded the award's grade. Stylized wings extended from either side of the wreath. Unusually for Hungarian clasps, it was attached by a central screw.

The Danube Flotilla issued its own proficiency clasp graded one to three and coloured: gold, silver and bronze. It featured a red star with white number shield below behind which was two crossed anchors, from which extended oak leaves.

(**Above**) Hungarian People's Army early issue Proficiency Clasp second class for an Army Engineer. The blue field is covered by a thick plastic coating which lends it a more substantial look than the later variants.

(**Above**) Hungarian People's Army Proficiency Clasps assigned to a variety of services and trades.

(**Below**) Hungarian People's Army (top to bottom): Sky Diver Proficiency Clasp. An alternative version existed with a descending parachute suspended above the central wreath; Armoured Vehicle Proficiency Clasp. This clasp is almost identical to a version issued by the USSR. The chief differences are a reduction in the quality of manufacture and attachment via a pin rather than screw post.

(**Below**) Hungarian People's Army late-issue Proficiency Clasp second class for airborne Troops. Rather than a thick plastic coating this version has had a gloss lacquer applied to the blue field.

Romania

Romania produced a modest but attractive range of clasps. The RPR issued the customary tank and signals clasps graded one through to three, crowned with the RPR Socialist star. The RSR dispensed with the tank clasp (replacing it with a numbered proficiency badge) but did retain the signals clasp, the only amendment to which was the replacement of the RPR star with that of the RSR coat-of-arms. The air force produced a more varied range of clasps. Those of the RPR featured a circular cockade from which extended naturalistic wings backed by a variety of emblems: crossed swords (pilot and navigator), parachute (airborne), hammer and wrench (flight engineer). The RSR continued the use of these clasps except the cockade was replaced by the RSR coat-of-arms. A triangle was placed beneath the centre of the clasp and recorded the relevant grade: one, two, three, or unclassified.

DDR

The DDR issued its first set of clasps between 1958 and 1967. These original clasps were of a small size when compared to later issues. They featured a central wreath within which was a visual representation: tank (armour), ship (navy), dog's head (border guard dog handler) and so on. At the top of the wreath was the national flag with the clasp's grade recorded at its base (either M for master, I, II or III). All had a screw attachment. The most common type is the dog handler because it was issued from 1966 to 1990. The first issue parachute clasp was awarded from 1960 to 1963. Those with a central screw were Soviet made, while those with twin screws (one on each arm of the wings) were German made. It featured a central oval with a descending parachute within it. A diamond at the top of the wreath contained the national flag while the base recorded the grade. The stylized wings extending from the wreath were of a squarer design than those found on other clasps.

Between 1963 and 1985 a second series of clasps was produced. These were larger than the ones they replaced. They featured oak leaf arms flanking a central square and were restricted to general proficiency (state coat-of-arms), armour, navy, parachute, air force pilot, flight engineer and technical – all graded from I down to III, which was recorded at the top of the central square. Early versions were of solid brass, while the later issues were made of stamped metal. Both types featured twin screw attachments.

From 1987 to 1990 a third series of clasps was produced. These were gold in colour and once again ranged from master down to III. They featured an oval oak wreath with a coloured field and branch-of-service motif and oval grade plate. The range was extended to include all types of soldier and, although only issued for three years, very few should be considered rare. However, they do often command good prices as they have always managed to attract a significant level of interest.

(Above) RPR Romanian People's Army Armoured Crewman Proficiency Clasp third class. Clearly a regional variation of the Soviet proficiency clasp. However, the Romanian example does differ in that it is a two-piece construction with the central portion of the badge separately applied.

(Above) RSR Romanian People's Army Signals Proficiency Clasp third class.

(Above) DDR National People's Army first type Parachute Proficiency Clasp.

(Right) DDR National People's Army 1987 last issue Armoured Crewman Proficiency Clasp second class.

Miscellaneous

(**Above**) USSR Soviet Armed Forces Commemorative Good Memory of the Soviet Armed Forces Badges (left to right): painted aluminium with 50th Anniversary of the Red Army hanger, painted aluminium issue badge with alternative design; first issue superior quality painted and enamelled brass.

Anniversary and Celebration Badges

Time validates all things and the Socialist Governments of the Eastern Bloc, always keen to stress their own validity, frequently exploited every celebration available to them. Every passing year helped to reinforce the overriding message that socialism was here to stay so do not try to resist the dictatorship of the people. Consequently, for the Warsaw Pact collector, the most common unqualified badges to be encountered are those recording an anniversary or other celebration. This common status, however, is only applicable when the badges are viewed as a collective. When viewed individually these badges are much less common as many of them were only issued once and had a production run of less than a year. They can also be divided into a number of specific subcategories, which makes many of them even rarer than they at first appear. As such, they often command a great deal of interest amongst collectors in-the-know and can gain some of the highest prices paid for non-combat awards of this era.

(**Above**) CSSR Czechoslovakian People's Army Warsaw Pact Annual Joint Manoeuvres Participants Commemorative Badge for the 1972 war games operation 'Shield'.

Annual Manoeuvres and Joint Exercises

Every year contingents from each of the Pact nations would congregate within a host country and stage annual manoeuvres. This act was celebrated by the issuing of a commemorative badge, produced by the host nation. There was no fixed design and its appearance was generally unique to that particular year; although certain reoccurring elements were often present, which can help with identifying this type of badge: name of the exercise (usually 'shield' or the location where the manoeuvres took place), flags of the attendant nations and the year. The quality and method of manufacture depended on the traditions and economic condition of the host nation and so no further generalizations can be made as to what to expect from this type of badge.

Similar badges were also produced to celebrate smaller scale manoeuvres, which took place between neighbouring states. Again, the host nation assumed the responsibility (and presumably the cost) for the design and production of the badge. They are rarer than the full-scale manoeuvres, but they do not seem to have acquired the same level of appreciation or value. The final badge to feature within this classification was the Good Memory of the Soviet Armed Forces of the USSR Badge. It was issued by the USSR to officers and senior ranking members of foreign delegations who had taken part in, or been allowed to observe, military manoeuvres. Unlike the annual Pact manoeuvres these were not necessarily produced to celebrate a single event but were of a more generic type issued at different times for a number of years. However, variations did occur and one such example is when a

(**Above**) CSSR Czechoslovakian People's Army Warsaw Pact Annual Joint Manoeuvres Participants Commemorative Badge for the 1984 war games operation 'Shield'. Standard painted aluminium version in low relief.

(**Right**) CSSR Czechoslovakian People's Army Warsaw Pact Annual Joint Manoeuvres Participants Commemorative Badge for the 1984 war games operation 'Shield'. Rare alternative version with reversed colours in high relief.

59

(Above) Hungarian People's Army and Poland Participants Commemorative Badges for small-scale manoeuvres (left to right): Hungary, Danube 1985; Poland, Tarcza 1976.

(Above) USSR Soviet Armed Forces Red Army Commemorative Day Pin. Cheap painted aluminium badges of this type are very common and were not exclusively worn by members of the Armed Forces.

fifty pendant was added to the badge in order to record the Soviet Armed Forces' Fiftieth Birthday. Another such example was when the manufacture of the badge went from brass and enamel over to painted aluminium. They are all quite easy to identify because, although the design did change from time to time, the inscription always remained the same.

Anniversaries

The Soviet Union issued commemorative medals for most of its major military victories and armed forces' birthdays, which was also a tradition copied by most of the other Pact nations. The DDR, however, celebrated its national landmarks through the issuing of badges with medals more commonly recording length of service. As can have been expected, World War II was tactfully avoided for the greater part, but the creation of the DDR and the NVA were anniversaries actively celebrated. On a five-yearly basis the NVA celebrated its birth with a commemorative badge and, at slightly less intervals, also the creation of the Warsaw Pact. The design of each badge varied from year to year, but as a general rule they were all of a fairly inexpensive type – usually painted aluminium. The only consistent exception appears to have been the Worker's Militia. They produced badges to celebrate their twentieth, twenty-fifth, thirtieth and thirty-fifth anniversaries in a range of good-quality metals. The only thing that has since let them down is the unfortunate DDR habit of lacquering badges with gloss or plastic coatings.

Anniversaries commonly celebrated by the Soviet Union via the issuing of a badge were those celebrating the formation of individual units, usually referred to as veterans' badges. Most commonly this type of badge was a two-piece construction made of painted aluminium with a ring suspension that lent it the appearance of a medal, although more conventional badge designs were also issued. Naval surface craft and submarines produced crewmembers badges, while training academies and military schools often commissioned badges to celebrate their individual anniversaries, most often in multiples of five or ten. Other Pact nations did the same to varying degrees of interest.

(Left) DDR National People's Army 20th and 25th Anniversary Badges. Possibly more so than any other Pact nation, the DDR rarely missed an opportunity to celebrate a key date. Very many anniversary badges of this type were produced, although their frequency has not detracted from their value as they are all highly collectable.

(Below) RSR Romanian People's Army Pilot Training School Commemorative Badge.

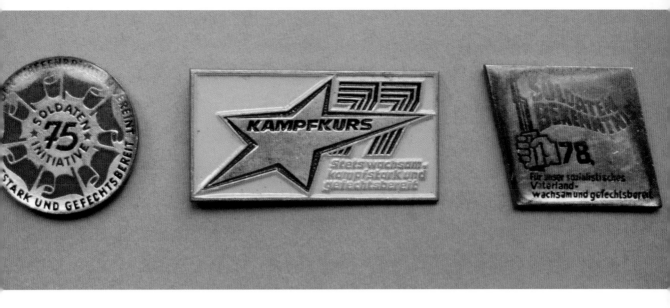

(Above) DDR National People's Army Annual Manoeuvres Participants Commemorative Badges. A selection of badges to celebrate participation in the annual war games exercises organised by the NVA.

(Above) Hungarian People's Army. A selection of commemorative shields issued to troops as keep-sakes.

(Above) Hungary Worker's Militia 25th Anniversary Commemorative 'medal'. Such medallion-type badges were a common feature of the Warsaw Pact. Very often they were used to commemorate various anniversaries and memorial dates.

(Above) USSR Soviet Armed Forces Soviet Navy Badges (top): Long Voyage surface craft; Parachute. Interestingly, the only connection to the sea that it has is the use of dolphins in its design; Long Voyage submarine (middle) Long Voyage surface craft; Long Voyage surface craft; Long Voyage submarine; (bottom): Long Voyage surface craft; submarine commemorative; Long Voyage submarine.

Soviet Navy Long Voyage

There is room to mention this particular type of naval badge as it was often awarded to members of the Soviet Naval Infantry. As the title suggests, this badge was issued for having undergone a long journey on board ship (worth recording as many journeys took place in potentially hostile water). The badge featured the Soviet Navy flag, beneath which sailed a medium-class ship. Below the vessel was a brass wreath and red inscription. Early examples date from the 1960s and were made of hollow or solid cast brass and enamel. The vessel was most often plated with silver-gilt highlights. They could be attached by either a pin or a screw.

During the 1970s a slightly cheaper version of brass and gloss paint was employed. For a brief period in the 1980s, brass and enamel badges returned, although they differed from earlier examples by using orange in place of red, being of a slightly larger design and having a smooth finish. These are the rarest badges of this standard type and so command the highest prices. In general terms, though, it is worth noting that the submarine version is significantly scarcer than the surface vessel badge. On rare occasions these badges were issued for specific voyages, such as the Soviet Navy's official visit to the UK in 1956. Other similar badges were produced as crew-member badges, the long voyage inscription being replaced by the name of the ship. These are less common than the long voyage badge, but unless they record a specific voyage or anniversary they are not to be considered as significantly rare.

(Above) USSR Soviet Armed Forces Soviet Navy Crewman Badge 'Albatros'.

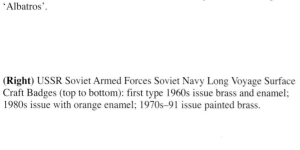

(Right) USSR Soviet Armed Forces Soviet Navy Long Voyage Surface Craft Badges (top to bottom): first type 1960s issue brass and enamel; 1980s issue with orange enamel; 1970s–91 issue painted brass.

(Above) USSR Soviet Armed Forces Soviet Navy (top): Crewman Badge; Crewman Badge: Submarine Commemorative; (middle): Surface Craft Commemorative; Coastal Border Guard; Submarine Crewman Badge; (bottom): Marine Diver Qualification Badge; late issue Soviet Navy Extended Service Clasp; Submarine Crewman Badge, late issue painted aluminium.

(Above) USSR Armed Forces KGB Coastal Border Guard Crewman Badge. Note how the bottom stripe of the flag is coloured green instead of the usual blue.

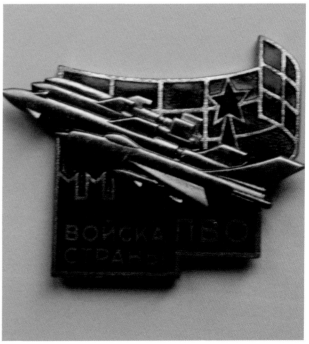

(Above) CSSR Czechoslovakian People's Army. Badge to Commemorate Soviet–Czechoslovakian Friendship. Possibly not the most popular badge issued after the Soviet invasion of 1968, it was certainly a common badge.

(Above) USSR Soviet Armed Forces Air Force Air Defence Badge. A good-quality badge made from enamelled brass and white metal. A two-piece construction with a screw post attachment. An attractive and well-made badge which is, surprisingly, not too uncommon.

Youth Pins

The best soldiers were not necessarily the bravest or the most intelligent but those who had undertaken the correct political training. For this reason, membership of a political youth organization prior to military service was something to be advertised and it was not uncommon for Pact soldiers to wear youth pins on their tunics. The most basic type was the membership pin. For the USSR it was a small, red flag within which was contained the side profile of Lenin and the organization's initials below *Komsomol*. Always of good quality, the military version had a screw attachment. The red detail on the obverse was either enamel or a plastic enamel-effect gloss. (Early examples from the 1950s featured just a star and initials within the flag.) It was worn at all times on the wearer's left-hand side in line with the second button down from the collar, or below the medals when on parade. In addition, the *Komsomol* awarded badges for military valour or military excellence, although they are significantly rarer, whereas the standard membership pin was then, and still is, very common.

The other Pact nations tended to award graded pins for excellence (by which they meant political knowledge and aptitude). These were most frequently graded gold, silver and bronze. The best examples come from the DDR, where the Free German Youth (FDJ) organization issued a graded pin featuring the side profiles of Marx, Engels and Lenin for Sound Knowledge. At the time of issue they were highly regarded, their order of precedence on military tunics came before that of the Army Bester Badge, but their frequent survival on the collector's market today has diminished their appeal. The same applies to the other Pact nations and these youth pins can be acquired very easily with the exception of the Hungarian Sagvari Endre Badge. This award was as highly regarded as the FDJ Sound Knowledge Badge and was made of good-quality brass and enamel with a gold portrait of Socialist martyr Sagvari (who was killed in 1944).

(Above) USSR Soviet Armed Forces Military Pattern *Komsomol* Members Pin. The wearing of this pin on the uniform demonstrated membership of the major Soviet youth organization – *Komsomol*.

(Above) FDJ (Free German Youth) pins issued for Sound Knowledge in gold, silver and bronze classes. These badges, although youth pins, were highly placed on military uniforms. Possibly more so than any other Pact nation, the DDR recognized the importance of political reliability when filling the ranks of its army and it paid a soldier to advertise their membership of a political organization.

Bibliography

Publications

Bonds, Ray (ed.), *The Soviet War Machine* (Hamlyn, 1976)

Lewis, William, J., *The Warsaw Pact: Arms, Doctrine, and Strategy* (Institute for Foreign Policy Analysis Book, 1982)

Rottman, Gordon, *Warsaw Pact Ground Forces* (Osprey, 1987)

Stevens, Fred et al., *Weapons and Uniforms of the USSR* (Purnell and Sons LTD, 1975)

Urban, Mark, L., *Soviet Land Power* (Ian Allan Ltd, 1984)

Von Pivka, Otto, *The Armies of Europe Today* (Osprey, 1974)

Wiener, Friedrich, *Army, Navy & Air Force Uniforms of the Warsaw Pact* (A&AP, 1978)

Zaloga, Steven, J., *Inside the Soviet Army Today* (Osprey, 1987)

Zaloga, Steven, J., *Soviet Bloc Elite Forces* (Osprey, 1985)

Websites

www.collectrussia.com

www.fleece-militaria.com

www.gowen-militaria.com